*Becoming the Villainess*

# Becoming the
# Villainess

Jeannine Hall Gailey

STEEL TOE BOOKS
BOWLING GREEN, KENTUCKY

Book Design by Joelean Copeland

Cover Design by Michaela Eaves

Steel Toe Books
Department of English
135 Cherry Hall
Western Kentucky University
1 Big Red Way
Bowling Green, KY 42101-3576

The author wishes to give special thanks:

> To my husband, Glenn Gailey, for all his support and encouragement, and especially all those trips to the post office in the rain.

> To my parents, Dr. Ernest and Bettie Hall, for all their love and support, and to my little brother, Michael Hall, for his advice in all things relating to comic books and video games.

> To Kim Addonizio, Marvin Bell, Dorianne Laux, Ilya Kaminsky, Don Bogen, and Andrew Hudgins, who all helped immensely with the poems that appear in this book.

> To Kelli Russell Agodon, Ronda Broatch, Janet Knox, Jenifer Lawrence, Natasha Moni, and Annette Spaulding-Convy for their years of friendship and feedback.

> Thanks to Lisa Galloway and Steven Schroeder for their comments on this manuscript.

> Special thanks also to Colleen McElroy and John Drury.

> To Tom C. Hunley, for his help and patience.

> To the artist of the cover work, Michaela Eaves: thanks for your unique vision and all your hard work.

# TABLE OF CONTENTS

## I. Origins

## II. Superpower

## III. Character Arc

*For Bettie Corinne Hall*

# I. Origins

## Alice in Darkness

Forget tears. Chasing
white animals with timepieces
in this drug-trip landscape
can only lead to more of same.
Hedgehogs, playing cards, paintbrushes:
full of undisclosed danger.
Didn't your mother tell you
not to kiss strangers?
That Cheshire smile shouldn't fool you.
Pull your skirt down.
Your nails are growing so fast
you're hardly human.
Alice, fight your version of Bedlam
as long as you can.
Sleep the sweet dream away
from that gooey looking glass, or mushrooms,
or the fear of your own body.
Forget what the night tastes like.
Stop wondering through the shadows,
holding your neck out
for the slice of the axe.

## Breathing in the Asthma Capital

In Knoxville two miles from Oak Ridge
I grew up with a yard of lilacs

despite stray dogs, stray cars jackknifed into lawns

the lilacs press their tiny mouths
cool and faded
to my fingertips

despite crushed cigarettes and smells of tar

lilac branches climb uncertain
above asparagus, moss, strawberry leaves
they rise like watery flames out of red clay

despite seasons of radioactive snow

despite spring shedding its wreckage
on rotting house frames, gravel roads
on overturned crates of mangoes on I-75

the lilacs go on burning
radiant
and thick against a grey May sky.

# Female Comic Book Superheroes

are always fighting evil in a thong,
pulsing techno soundtrack in the background
as their tiny ankles thwack

against the bulk of male thugs.
They have names like Buffy, Elektra, or Storm
but excel in code decryption, Egyptology, and pyrotechnics.

They pout when tortured, but always escape just in time,
still impeccable in lip gloss and pointy-toed boots,
to rescue male partners, love interests, or fathers.

Impossible chests burst out of tight leather jackets,
from which they extract the hidden scroll, antidote, or dagger,
tousled hair covering one eye.

They return to their day jobs as forensic pathologists,
wearing their hair up and donning dainty glasses.
Of all the goddesses, these pneumatic heroines most

resemble Artemis, with her miniskirts and crossbow,
or Freya, with her giant gray cats.
Each has seen this apocalypse before.

See her perfect three-point landing on top of that chariot,
riding the silver moon into the horizon,
city crumbling around her heels.

## Leda's Mother Warns Her

Beware your face,
 your limbs, your walk:

gods see these
as invitations.

Beware of swans.
They may lift you

but you will fall.
Beware children

hatched from eggs,
unfledged and beautiful:

they will burn
cities to the ground.

Don't be seduced by the gods,
my daughter.

Though you break
into song beneath them

you will remain broken.

# Remembering Philomel

The professor asks, what is the scene here, class? The writer
(ah-vid, not oh-vid) here is so spare, implying violence in so few
words. Who do you think this character is? You can't write about
a character without imagining her surroundings in vivid detail. Tell
us the story from her point of view.

I can't. After the scene, I can't remember
anything. Why do I have to do this? I'm fine.
It's over. I do remember six—
my favorite library book was The Nightingale,
pictures of the jeweled robotic bird the emperor
preferred, and the gray one who never sang
a waltz, refused all command performances.
I loved the sense of triumph.

*Listen: I used to be exquisite, cool—*
*A brightness of skin, an affected grace,*
*appropriate beauty of a rapid princess.*
*But see, diminutive in drab gray now*
*I sing.*

Anger hung like smoke in my home,
between my mother and my father. At six
I knew. I tried to pet her yellow hair
smelling of nicotine and toffee, kiss her
read her my fairy tales to make her smile.

*I loved my older sister Procne, who*
*seemed smarter, better than me at all the games.*
*we used to play. I wanted to be grown-up, like her.*
*After she left, I used to walk the ocean every morning,*
*barefoot, watching, and when I finally saw her ship*
*slice through the horizon, there was no warning,*
*no cold horror clenched my stomach like a fist.*

*I thought my sister's husband elegant,*
*with a thin mouth. How grand he was,*
*and I not a little dazzled. What I could not*
*see was that he had already devised*
*his possession of me. Light, thin,*
*a wisp of sea blue eyes and a cloud of hair*
*a softness of limb and mouth—just beyond his reach*
*this is how I appeared to him*

We need the actual story about what happened to you, says the
professor. What are the details?

I can't remember exactly. I remember that night,
when my parents told me they were going
to a party together, I felt happy. They left me
with a favorite sitter, a neighbor—he was
friends with all the older girls around,
they'd say how cute he was, looking back I guess he was—
lanky and tan with a slow slack southern drawl

*Not a little afraid, when he took my*
*hand too tight, told me to trust him.*
*"Where is my sister?"*
*This is where I stop remembering in sentences.*
*Only fragments because growing up*
*in the right kind of family meant you*
*had no words for what he was doing.*

I don't get the drama here. Class, do you have a clear sense of
what is happening? Is he raping her? Is there penetration? Come
on, you need to give us a story.

Of course not uneasy, when he locked the doors,
asked me if my brothers were away for the night.
I told him I was cold, the basement clammy and

It smelled moldy, I complained. At six much
too young to suspect as he carefully switched on
a too-loud TV, as he began undressing

he told me to take off my pants. Thin little jeans, with
sunflowers on the pockets, a T-shirt to match, and
tiny pink underwear he was impatient with.
I was scared, crying quietly, and he told me to shut up.
I remember rough hands but that's it,

> *no details. Only the raw chafe of his body crushing me,*
> *his rutting moans, the smells of salt and rotted fish,*
> *the grating of unknown soil beneath me.*
> *Shoving himself into me until I bled,*
> *a red, frightening blood that seemed to excite him.*
> *Forcing his flesh in my mouth as my jaw ached,*
> *I thought he looked like a dying sheep.*
> *I thought of dying, then—floating away from him, from my body*
> *and so I did not taste the tears and bile on my lips*

Later, I wonder why, when I finally told her,
my mother said, "It is something we women
bear in secret."

That doesn't seem realistic, like something a mother would say.
Perhaps you could reword it?

> I couldn't push the story out,
> my mouth was filled with blood

> *I rearranged my dress and hair*
> *as he approached me when he was done.*
> *I choked if there were any gods in heaven*

> *He grabbed me and the knife he put to my face*
> *smelled cold. You won't be telling anyone he said*

Growling as if unsatiated, he let me go.
I chewed on my hair, as you better not tell your parents
when they get home he said. Why not I asked

*Kill me, I was sobbing over and over*
*when he cut my tongue off violent and quick.*
*It danced a little, the blood filled my mouth like a song*

I'll kill you if you tell anyone he said. So when
he smiled and accepted money from my dressed-up
mother, I told them I had had a good time.
For the first time my mouth was my enemy

*Unable to speak, I wove the ugly scenes shrunken*
*on pillows and coverlets*
*over and over, scenes no one could see.*

But Philomel's crime is eventually avenged. The gods did witness
the crime, had mercy on her. She is saved by the gods.

Not saved—changed, it's not the same thing.

ripping the chrysalis that was me
the good daughter, the pretty girl

If they clap their hands it will not matter.
In the silence a song of the new leaves.

## Okay, Ophelia

We've heard you were a victim.
Stop crouching in shadows, chewing your hair.

You can be graceful, not like a ballerina,
like a hedge of coral,

built up and eaten and worn down
yet alive, carving the rhythms of the seas.

You can be a threshing sledge,
new and sharp with many teeth.

## Playing Softball with Persephone

She throws that heavy globe
so that it sinks in the dirt
a gash in semisoft mud
around the shoe-crushed wildflowers
and the gnats ring her hair like a crown.

She looks right at me while she drinks Gatorade,
pulling her sweaty bangs up over her face
and her eyes like a whole field of forget-me-nots.

The ball rolls forward and she grabs it,
squeezes it like a ripe pomegranate, almost takes a bite,
then wipes her mouth on her dusty arm.

## *A Girl and Her Gun*

At seven, she learns to shoot a rifle
at camp. At first afraid
to lift it too close to her shoulder, worried
she won't hit the target.
First try, bull's-eye, a ribbon.
The smoke, the bang, the sharp taste of that first shot

still hang in her mind's eye.
Later, her mother shows her
how to load her father's .38 Special.
She says, "Once I shot my sister,
just with a BB gun, but still had to go
to the hospital. Don't point it at anyone,
ever, even if you're just playing."

At the shooting range she lines up
next to her older brother, who says
"If you really want to take someone out,
someone farther away,
a moving target,
a rifle's what you need."
Her brother's used to blasting aliens,
bad guys at the arcade.

When she gets old enough
to stay by herself, her mother
tells her if anyone breaks in, to get
out her father's gun. "That gun is an equalizer,"
she says. "And don't mess around.
If you're going to shoot, aim for the chest
and shoot to kill."

At thirteen, she's never shot a thing
only a paper target, still weeps when the boys

try to hit birds or even an ugly possum.
Still too young to imagine
the need to aim at someone coming at her,
to steady her gaze at heart-level,
reach the trigger, squeeze.

## II. Superpower

## Female Comic Book Superheroes II:
## When Catholic School Girls Strike Back

In one moment, the cluster of plaid
uniforms, fists and ankles,
descend on the now-hapless criminal:
a horde of angry green bees.

When later interviewed, one girl stated: "Our parents were real proud."

Imagine every girl that walks alone
down a dark alley filled
with her own avenging angels:
feathers flying, fury like dust cudgels.

## Wonder Woman Dreams of the Amazon

I miss the tropes of Paradise—green vines
roped around wrists, jasmine coronets,
the improbably misty clothing of my tribe.

I dream of the land where they celebrated
my birth, named me after their patron Goddess.
I was to be a warrior for their kind.

I miss my mother, Hippolyta.
In my dreams she wraps me tightly
again in the American flag,

warning me, cling to your bracelets,
your magic lasso. Don't be a fool for men.
She's always lecturing me, telling me

not to leave her. Sometimes she changes
into a doe, and I see my father
shooting her, her blood. Sometimes,

in these dreams, it is me who shoots her.
My daily transformation
from prim kitten-bowed suit to bustier

with red-white-and-blue stars
is less disturbing. The invisible jet
makes for clean escapes.

The animals are my spies and allies;
inexplicably, snow-feathered doves
appear in my hands. I capture Nazis

and Martians with boomerang grace.
When I turn and turn, the music plays louder,
the glow around me burns white-hot,

I become everything I was born to be,
the dreams of the mother,
the threat of the father.

## In the Faces of Lichtenstein's Women

We see our own faces, drawn near,
smiling tightly.

We do not quite mouth
the black letters hanging in balloons.

Our eyes water
with the brightness of your gaze.

Crayon-yellow hair with the curves of a fifties 'Vette
severed by the edge of the frame.

(This is a real scene.)
Towers rise sharp like Superman's Metropolis;

a moon hangs like a yellow eye,
malevolent and certain of its permanence.

In this world,
the noise from a gun floats forever.

## Amazon Women on the Moon

In the green, green light
we wait for you, entangled in silver
nightclothes and our long white hair.
We know you are coming.
Our songs travel through the air to you,
like clouds of radiant dust indifferent to gravity.

You, you race from your spaceship,
helmet under arm, confident
you will win over our queen.
(She is the one in thigh-high pleather boots,
a sign of royalty.)

Without question we feed you
and your crew. We repair your pathetic
engine with our glamour, our technologies.
We offer you a glass of something foaming and neon,
but you wave it away, laugh,
and ask instead for a kiss.

There is nothing you can give us in return,
we know that already. You've forgotten
your shoes and your ray gun. We know soon
you will board your broken ship,
leave us alone, as usual,
terrible and glowing in our lunar skins
to sing brilliantly to an eclipsed blue earth.

## When Red Becomes the Wolf

In my dream you brought me fried bologna sandwiches.
"But wait," you said, "You don't even like bologna."
I wolfed them down without answering.

I have never owned a red cape,
that's asking for trouble, I knew.
In the forest by your house,

I met someone gathering wood. "Nice axe,"
I said before wandering further.
I was obtaining samples for my botany class.

How many daisies make a statistic?
I thought of Persephone, her dark gash
that allowed Hades passage. Which flower?

I was hungry, and tired. I entered someone's
cottage, it was dark, and there was an old woman.
I volunteered to take her to get her hair done.

Alone, I mentioned I was born under the sign
of Lupus. "No," she corrected, "Lupae."
Later, eating sandwiches, we discussed you

and also whether I could wear her fur coat.
"It makes you look feral, with your green eyes,"
she said. Oh grandmother, what a big mouth you have.

# Mongolian Cow Sour Sour Yogurt Super Girl

These are the finalists: a tomboy, a baby doll, a glamour girl, a
punk rocker.
They crowd onto a tiny stage and an ad for Johnson's baby wipes
flashes on screen behind them.  210 million viewers.

The punk rocker sings a song in English. The judge says,
"You should have trusted the mother
tongue." She is eliminated in the next round.

One woman spent three month's salary
following the contest from town to town.
Each time she was rejected in the first round.

Some girls traveled fifteen hours by bus,
stood another two days in line. Even third place
means a spot in the sun, ad deals, maybe modeling.

"Our motto," says the contest runner,
is: "If you want to sing, sing."
In the lineup of girls dreaming of instant fame,

of smiling for the camera, taut stomach gleaming,
a coil of craving for more, for better,
the dangerous growl of newborn desire.

## Spy Girls

always get their fiancés killed
in the very first scene.
A femme fatale can't also be
a loving wife and mother.
So she becomes a workaholic
to get over Steve, Jeff, or Lance,
sliding down elevator chutes
cutting through plate glass windows
carefully cracking the codes of illegal governments
dressed in formfitting rubber suits and blue wigs.
Temporarily blinded with acid spray
and shot through a shoulder and thigh,
she still manages to somersault over the wall
to grab the bars of the helicopter
just as it lifts off
secrets of nuclear fission in a disk
tucked in her lace-up boots,
keeping the world safe
from people just like her.
At night, she dreams of rescue,
of blending in with the crowd
of being one more girl
who eats ice cream for dinner
whose purse is not full of explosives.

# Dirge for a Video Game Heroine: On Dying Again

It should get less painful, over time—
death by drowning, death by demon bite—
but it doesn't. And each time there is that moment
of melancholy accorded to me by my creator,

the moment my limbs collapse around me,
hair, in a long braid, falling, coiled, at last,
the moment I sigh or let out a choked, guttural "Urghhh…"
depending on whether I was drained of blood

by an undead creature or shot off a cliff
and then the scene around me fades to black.
It is my job, after all, kill or be killed
along with changing outfits unseen between levels,

(kimono? catsuit? chain mail minidress?)
nimbly switching from blade to Uzi,
slaying assailants with increasing speed and accuracy.
And twenty seconds later (mourning period over)

I am back, ready to die again on the whim of the joystick.
One moment, able to somersault over mummies
and scramble between swinging axes; the next, unable
to extract myself from the poisonous slime pit, and so

the last you'll see of me is my mouth making its "O" of surprise,
my eyes closing as if to sleep—this time, maybe, forever.

# III. Character Arc

# My Little Brother, In Parts

*Part 1: Assassins*

At thirteen, my brother
dreams of becoming a paid assassin.
He mimics violence—tries a roundhouse kick,
barely missing my head, slices an imagined machete,
his lips puckered to exhale explosions.
He sleeps with knives under his pillow.
His eyes remain trained on his computer,
even as we have a conversation.
I watch his little character somersault,
shoot at menacing aliens. "Here, try" he says.
I squeeze the trigger button once, again,
aiming the lasers with terrifying ease,
splattering green extraterrestrial goo
over the buzzing electronic landscape.

*Part II: Chinese Stars*

My brother was caught on the bus today
with Chinese stars, little metal disks
with cunning grooves
designed to catch in flesh.

He carries them in the inside pockets
of his jacket and pants. He brags
he's gotten them through airport customs—twice.
Now I have to drive him to school.

He offers to show me how to throw them.
My brother puts the jagged circle in my hand,
showing me how to hold them so I don't cut myself,
and moves my elbow.

The motion's just like fly-fishing,
graceful and clean. The campy red dragon
smiles back at me from the face of the star,
jaws deep in maple bark.

## Little Cinder

Girl, they can't understand you.
You rise from the ash-heap in a blaze
and only then do they recognize you
as their one true love.

While you pray beneath your mother's
tree you carve a phoenix into your palm
with a hazel twig and coal;
every night she devours more of you.

You used to believe in angels.
Now you believe in the makeover;
if you can't get the grime off your face
and your foot into a size six heel

who will ever bother to notice you?
The kettle and the broom sear in your grasp,
snap into fragments. The turtledoves sing,
"There's blood within the shoe."

You deserve the palace, you think, as you signal
the pigeons to attack, approve the barrel filled with red-hot nails.
Its great hearth beckons, and the prince's flag
rises crimson as the angry sun.

He will love you for the heat you generate,
for the flames you ignite around you,
though he encase your tiny feet in glass
to keep them from scorching the ground.

## While Reading Glamour in a Dark Age

A model trips footloose in yellow satin
in an elevator filled with green balloons.
Across from me in a bus a child is crying,
her mouth muffled with a plastic starfish.

The obsidian edge of a limousine
blurs the mink shrugs of two starlets
named Jennifer, the latest comets
speeding their way through Hollywood,

Paris, New York. Their trails of flame
descend in a tango of dust. I grow older.
I watch a woman whose lipstick is creeping
outward. She grips the wrench in her lap

like a sword. She mutters something
that might be song lyrics, "We used
to ride through the streets carrying
gray guitars." The late afternoon light

falls on the glossy pages. Tomorrow
will come soon, and I will keep an army
of bracelets, new soft drinks, shampoos
close to my ear as I sleep.

## Allerleirauh Reveals Her True Self to the Prince

I'd rather be mistaken for an animal.
If you knew what I ran from,
how my mother cursed me with golden hair, this face.

She left me a father obsessed with her image.
I fear your eyes, as I feared his.
This coat offers shelter.

So you put me to work in your kitchen, assumed
I was a magical beast, or a lunatic child,
and I kept dropping hints in your soup:

one night, a tiny spinning wheel,
the next night, a gold ring,
trying to tell you who I used to be.

I can dance just as I used to dance,
in dresses shining as the stars,
in dresses pale as the moon,

but I am not the same princess.
In older stories, where I am a saint,
I never even get to the safety of you.

My disguises fail. I am found by my father.
Sometimes, he cuts off my hands;
other times, he cuts out my tongue.

## Persephone and the Prince Meet Over Drinks

At first I thought, Daddy?
squinting in the shadows when I saw his face,
alone at the bar.
So many similarities to the picture
mother keeps on the mantel,
that squared jaw, those cold grey eyes.

His ravishing grin drew me in,
the way he treated me like a grown-up.
He bought me cocktails, whispers
of pomegranate in the bottom of the glass.
(How many is this? Four? Five? Six?)
I laughed and laughed, though he wasn't joking.

And so what if, at the end of this story,
with a ring on my finger and a castle
to boot, you find out that my prince
is prince of nothing but darkness?
I knew what I was doing.
I was prepared for a long dance with death.

## The Snow Queen

You tell yourself he only left you for her
because of the wicked shard of glass in his eye,
but the truth is, every man wants an ice princess.
The truth is, you're too easy to get used to—

your sloppy warmth, the heat from your skin
fresh from the garden—it's too much for him.
He'd rather marvel at her tedious snowflakes,
caress her frosted hair, basking in that cold gaze,

that veneer of symmetry. So you wander
around town like an idiot, forgetting
even your shoes. The boys there
are all still in awe of her. "Did you see

that thing she was driving?" they keep asking,
You set off to bring him back, not thinking
you are the last person he wants to see.
"He's trapped in that ice castle" you murmur,

"He needs to be rescued." Dogged, you follow
the tiny shards of glass, and their sparkle.
And when you finally find him, dark with cold
from her brutal kisses, he doesn't even

recognize you. You stop blaming the shard
in his eye; how can you rescue a man
whose heart, transfixed by skeletal crystal,
craves the bruising of frost?

## Philomel's Rape

You are smaller than you used to be, more fearful.
Your heart beats faster, trembles
beneath the weight of your former body.
All you are left with is the naming, "Tereu, Tereu"
This conversion was not of your choosing,

and the somewhat tenuous "gift," your song,
not as healing as you hoped.
Your sister, the swallow, forgets,
sings easily in the spring sunshine.
But you—you never change your tune—
it hangs in the air like honey, but stings the heart.

I think you memorized it before the final change,
before you regained a tiny black tongue,
back when you had your voice stolen

so now you go on, stubborn,
with this music that splinters atoms,
transforms matter in its path.
All around you fall leaves and petals
like a thousand tongues repeating "Stay Alive."

## Persephone's in Seattle

You haven't heard? She got married
and moved away. Just like that.
She met him one day
picking up flowers for a friend in the hospital.

He pulled up in a huge black Cadillac
and offered to drive.
She never made it to that hospital. She says,
now, it was dinner that seduced her,

she always was a sucker for a good fruit plate.
Her husband? He treats her okay, she says —
the last time I saw her, she was dripping
in jewelry and couture. The rain gets to her,

sometimes, and she's alone a lot.
She complains about the long winters,
but says the spring makes it all worth
while—imagine bleeding hearts,

wild poppies,  fuchsias,
pink and white camellias. Of course,
he bought her acres of gardens, but even he
can't buy her more sunlight.

She says she misses her mother most of all.
(That's Demeter, remember, who lives down the street,
looks great for her age?)
When she visits here each summer,

you'll notice she leaves him at home,
mentions something about his job,
busy season. She doesn't invite us to visit.
I think the move's been hard on her.

She's ghost white underneath
all that lipstick,
and rocks, unsteady,
as she tends her mother's garden.

## Pretty, Popular

She smiled so much her jaw ached.
Beneath tight jeans and Benetton sweater
her body woke, hopeful, every night.
She read books no one thought she
could understand—*Anna Karenina*, Victor Hugo.
During the day she spun, kicking
out of her cocoon with tasteful, pointed flats;
you never guessed.

In this photo, her hair is almost silver.
Her irises ringed in silver, too, their blue
mirror-like, and everyone sees themselves
inside, that's what they liked.
Her fingers moved like feathers, and you
wanted her to whisper your name alone.
Her cheeks seem hungrier now.

Here, in real life, her steps are brisker,
she moves everyone around her like game pieces,
here the children, there the husband and friends. Forget nostalgia.
Now is the time for her to become what she intended,
someone who *does things*, not just
ankle and thigh and neckline,
the soft, lovely tilt of her head.

You saw her at the bank,
gripping her checkbook like a knife,
holding a pen in teeth worn down,
all those years of smiling,
bone against bone.

## The Selkie Wife's Daughter

I always wondered why she sang so strangely
at the spinning wheel, why her eyes held all
the mourning of the darkest sea. And why
she held me away,

as if afraid of my skin, why my feet and
hands were webbed with translucent sea-skin.
I used to bring her armfuls of yellow
water iris to almost

see her smile. I wondered why father
never let me swim out against the waves,
never let her walk the shores alone.
He feared she might

disappear like a snatched breath on every
angry tide. And when I found the skin,
by accident, beneath the kindling, its fur
mottled as the moors

in summer, soft as milk in my twelve-year-old
hands, I brought it straight to her. I hoped
she might smile again. I couldn't guess
she might hold me close,

then shrug on that magic seal coat and swim
quickly away, enchantment broken, transformation
complete. She never saw me, waving frantic
from the shore.

So that's what she left me—webbed fingers
and toes, a lonely father, the stench of salt
and seaweed, the knowledge she had never
been herself with me.

# Cinderella at the Car Dealership

Let me get my manager,
the prince kept saying,
while Ella propped her tiny feet up
against the salesman's chair.

One shiny coach after another
kept appearing, one driven by mice,
another made of pumpkin.
(Environmentally sound.)

Let me see the 600 SL Deluxe,
she narrowed her eyes, her earrings
twinkling like glass.
She drove it up against the curb,

ran red lights, drove faster,
and the moon shone so bright her skull
glowed beneath her skin.
The frightened prince handed her

a contract, promised zero percent,
lifetime warranties.
She signed her name in blood,
and in the sky, doves scattered like vermin.

## Femme Fatale

Even our names sound delicious:
Pandora, Delilah, Bathsheba, Lola, Gilda

They speak of us in the language of pastries –
cream puff, tart, cupcake

They drool over us, put their hands in our bodies
*Oh honey, Oh sugar*
as if plunging into layers of white meringue

We dissolve behind veils and trench coats
our faces soon dimming
the whiskey of their tongues already forgotten

Around us the scent of orchids and tobacco flowers
bruised and senescent
blooms into the night air, thick with gunfire

# IV. Dark Phoenix, Rising

## The Villainess

resembles your mother, at least around the eyes—
treacherous, limpid and seal-like.
Inevitably handsome as a lioness, she
commands ranks, smokes cigarettes,
wears fur, has sex without apologizing.
Sometimes, she looks just like you,
but with crow's feet, more tattoos and better lingerie.

She conjures dragons or viruses,
she can lie easily to police or to you.
And you must love her, though she betrays you in a heartbeat.
You keep accepting the poisoned comb, the spinning wheel,
with open, pale hands.

## Keep Your Eye on the Swallow

This is not what you wanted to see:
a woman unkempt, blood from throat to fingertips.

You don't want to see
my hands on the knife,

their sordid work. Clawing those
blue robes, the jeweled reminders

of my marriage—you knew then
I could kill again, and not be sorry.

And though I have grown soft as feathers,
you shall not lay a hand on me.

My song is no invitation.

## Daphne, Older

Peel back my skin:
reveal hard fibers, bite marks,

scars from wind and rain.
Life is pain—I won't tell you

any different. Just that sometimes,
avoiding what you fear

isn't the answer. See? All these years
my branches sang with birds

and my leaves drank sunlight—
I haven't missed much.

My heartwood hardens slowly
over time—first, to the music, then, to the light.

## Becoming the Villainess

A girl—lovelocked, alone—wanders into a forest
where lions and wolves lie in wait.
The girl feeds them caramels from the pockets of her paper dress.
They follow like dogs.

Each day she weaves for twelve brothers, twelve golden shirts,
twelve pairs of slippers, twelve sets of golden mail.
She sleeps under olive trees, praying for rescue.
In her dreams doves fly in circles, crying out her name.

For a hundred years she is turned into a golden bird,
hung in a cage in a witch's castle. Her brothers
are all turned to stone. She cannot save them,
no matter how many witches she burns.

She weeps tears that cannot be heard
but turn to rubies when they hit the ground.
She lifted her hand against the light
and it became a feathered wing.

She learns the songs of mockingbirds, parakeets, pheasants.
She wanders into the forest more herself.
She speaks of her twelve stone brothers.
There is a dragon curled around eggs. There is a princess

who is also a white cat, and a tiny dog
she carries in a walnut shell.
She befriends a reindeer who speaks wisdom.
They are all in her corner. It seems unlikely now

that she will ever return home, remember what
it was like, her mother and father, the promises.
She will adopt a new costume,
set up shop in a witch's castle,

perhaps lure young princes and princesses
to herself, to cure what ails her—
her loneliness, her grandeur,
the way her heart has become a stone.

## Phoenix, Rising

She is complicated,
this empress of flame.

She's a martyr but no messiah,
though she may die and rise again.

No man can love completely
she who originates in ash-heaps,
poor cinder-bound, no matter how she shines.

She cannot align with good or evil;
she hovers above them both
and her wings remind us of death.

Her sunrise feathers singed,
she looks on the world with newborn eyes:

*you mortals, you breeders,*
*with your unending march of offspring.*

Her claws seize the skin
of a young goat; we turn away
from the greed of immortality.

The fire her grave, her grace and cradle,
we fear the span of her volcanic tears
but dream they will heal us.

Her cries sear the air with heat.
We cower in the shadow of her wings.

In her song, we hear our own prayers:
deliver us, deliver us.

## Job Requirements: *A Supervillain's Advice*

Grow up near a secret nuclear testing site.
Think Hanford, Washington. Oak Ridge,
Tennessee. North and South Dakota
are riddled with them. Your father—is he
an eccentric scientist of some sort? Did you
show early signs of a "supergenius" IQ?
Experience isolation from "normal" childhood
activities? (Multiple traumatic incidents welcome.)
Physical limitations, such as an unusual but poetic disease
or a deformity due to mutation, are preferred;
problems due to accidents involving powerful
new weaponry or interactions with superheroes
are also acceptable. (Develop flamboyant
criminal signatures. Adopt antisocial poses.)
A lack of respect for authority figures such as
world governments is a must.
Fashionable knack for skin-tight costumes
(masks, hooks, extra-long nails) considered a plus.
Study jujitsu or krav maga.
Practice creative problem solving;
for example, that lipstick could be poisoned,
that spiked heel a stabbing implement.
Remember, you are on the side
of the laws of thermodynamics. Entropy
is a measure of disorder.
Chaos, destruction, death: these are your instruments.
Use them wisely. You are no mere mortal.
Don't lose your cool if captured; chances are,
you can already control minds, bend metal to your whim,
produce, in your palms, fire.
In the end you are the reason we see the picture;
we mistrust the tedium of a string of sunny days.
We like to watch things crumble.

## The Snow Queen Explains

Hey, I didn't start out like this.
I enjoyed corned beef sandwiches,
good vodka. It started with sparkle—
one broken splinter in my foot, another in my finger.

Then I lived so far South the only snow
I'd seen was the shedding of magnolia,
a petal coat of white on the ground so thick
you had to kick through it.

I didn't notice how sounds had dampened,
how the summers with you became intolerable, sticky.
I lay in ice water baths, peeled off blankets,
nightgowns. You always complained
my hands were too cold anyway.

I moved North, started keeping pets with fur.
I enjoyed the way my new stilettos
pierced the fine layer of ice outside my door.
My Southern manners melted in the blank
face of so much snow.

A glassy film grew over my skin, perfecting.
My hair grew lighter without the touch
of sun. I built a palace from the remnants
of our life together—white car doors,
blocks of ice, mirrors, polished surfaces.

I dressed in white satin, white fox.
I carved swans in ice for company. After thirty,
I started wanting one boy after another—
I helped them with their homework and gave them toys.
Their bones stack up in the spare room.
Perhaps their girlfriends' tiny fists bang
on my palace door. I cannot hear them.

I don't think of you at all,
here, while my skin grows smoother
each year, while my hands and feet
become idols for the dead.

## Her Nerves

*"My nerves are bad tonight. Yes, bad."*
        —T.S. Eliot, *The Waste Land*

I surrounded myself with the safe, with the sane.
*"You know there's a history of mental illness in my family."*
I devoted myself to botany, to mazes, to the infinitesimal.
I married you to challenge my inevitable end—
my human tranquilizer.
You like my "little poems" but
I scare you when I rock myself over and over
saying I dreamed I killed you again,
I dreamed you killed me again,
and you couldn't stop the nightmares.

You liked it when I laughed at Plath,
sketched repeating uneven branches of starfish arms.

You are afraid—not just of me,
but what I see and hear that you don't—
the crusts of blood, slippery dirt-gorged voices.
You like it when I curse creatively,
hate it when paper piles like excrement around me.

Afraid our sloppy physicality
will tear at your maintained monastic cubes,
our "Siren Song," our red hair flaming into points.
You name our extremities as if decayed already,
the translucent hand,
the ankle frail as a twig.

# On Rubens' "Tereus Confronted with the Head of His Son Itylus"

You wonder "How can she offer up her own son's
head that way, practically flinging it at Tereus?"
This is revenge at its ugliest (not on the canvas
are the crimes of the father, his rape of Philomel,
her severed tongue, her long captivity in darkness.)
Procne's thinking only she married her sister's
rapist, gave him a son he did not deserve, little
Itylus. He begs her, "Mommy, don't" but she can't
hear him. Philomel's mute cries in her ears,
images of his father's hand on the knife in her eyes.
The murder is quick enough, but not the cooking;
it takes some thought to season a human stew.

           Light falls on the anguished
face of Tereus, the horrible secret of dinner just
dawning on him. According to the old story, Philomel
must be very young, twelve or thirteen, but Rubens
paints her, not a starved, beaten child but a creamy
milkmaid, bosom heaving, and Procne seems to be
losing her blouse. You feel the painter ogling the sisters,
sympathizing with the man who lost his child.
Why capture this moment? Why not the moment,
instead, of their flight, their sudden feathered
conversion, the exact second the blood on Procne's
dress stains the swallow's throat, when Philomel
finds her tongue once more in a nightingale's mouth?

## Conversation with the Stepmother, at the Wedding

I did the best that I could
and she turned out okay, didn't she?
It could have been a lot worse.
These shoes are killing me.

You don't understand how hard it was,
those greasy children
with their lentils, their field mice,
always playing with fire,

their clinging fingers wrapped
around locks of their mother's hair
or magic tree branches,
their grubby fists full of crumbs.

Hard to shake them loose
no matter how I comb their hair,
how many apples I feed them,
how many times I send them into the woods.

They never blame their father
who brought me here, to a house
full of strangers, where even the servants
worship images of the dead.

I say, make room for the new.

## The Changeling

I went to bed a secretary
but woke up a wolf,
clothes in shreds on the floor.

It is as you fear;
beneath the push-up bra,
the false set of eyelashes,
I am fundamentally "other."
I am not what I seem.

You will weep
when I disappear,
and never miss
the infant I stole
from your cradle.

## The Fairy Melusine's Reproach

They started calling me "witch"
after I built that first tower.

(*Overnight*, they whispered. *Must be magic.*
I taught them to keep bees, harvest haricots verts.
So much for gratitude.)

You didn't call me that
until after our tenth child,
each with some deformity:
blue and red eyes, giant ears,
long, threatening teeth.

My serpent nature, you said,
had corrupted your line.

I have every woman's curse—
hidden faerie insides.
I asked you to leave me alone
on Saturdays, during menstrual cycles, childbirth,
but you had to find out just why,
discovered I kept wings struggling under skin,
my legs replaced by a scaled dragon's tail,
gleaming in the light, in the water of my bath.
I should have known you knights were all alike,
claiming your thrall to enchanted monsters,
that you didn't have what it took to stick around.
I believed your lies, married beneath me.
You protested your love
while I built you castle after castle.

Now those castles are all that remain of us,
they litter Poitou, inspire legends.
The villagers carved my image into stones.

They say they've seen me keening round towers
sometimes a white spectre, sometimes in dragon form,
haunting fountains, presaging death.

Do I miss my legs, my human voice, you,
now that I've embraced my "darker half?"

No. When my sons became killers
it was your nature corrupting them, not mine.

## Case Studies in Revenge: Philomel Gives Some Advice

Trust me on this:
it turns to ash in your mouth.
(The cold air glitters above me.
I know what I know.
I've tasted blood.)

Like this one guy I knew
who was in love with this girl—
she was a tiny, 90-pound thing—
who was always getting beaten up
by her boyfriend, who was seven years older
and huge. So one night this guy
(maybe sixteen, ghost-white, only 140-pounds)
waits outside the bar
where the boyfriend works
as a bouncer.
He pulls the boyfriend into an alley,
pushes him to the ground,
stands over him with a metal bat.
Tells him he should kill him.
The boyfriend starts to cry
and the guy thinks, *Pathetic.*
He still wants to kill him
but won't. The boyfriend pleads,
promises he won't touch her
again. The girl later complains
to this same guy that her boyfriend
won't return her calls.
(The glint from empty beer cans
still stacked on her dresser.)

And this other girl I know,
there was a boy who picked on her

in school, called her names because
her mom shopped at the wrong stores,
she ate lunch with the wrong people,
had the wrong accent, etc.
She hated him and prayed
he would die. Two years later
he gets thrown through a windshield.
His best friend got leukemia.
She alone survives. Now she's afraid to hate,
but dresses impeccably.
(She grips the steering wheel
with white, white hands.)

And this other woman
she married young (in a white minidress
she holds white roses) a man
who bullied her, threw chairs at her
and she lived with it eleven years
and swore when her children were older
she would leave him. But then she fell
in love with him again
(his guitar music, his desire for only white cars)
and stayed another eleven years.
Her kids say she's nuts.

When I had my fill
of revenge, I began
making music. It tasted sweeter.
(The air's edge like a knife in my feathers.)

# V. The Final Frame

## She Escapes the Film Noir

I slip out the door,
wearing a raincoat as disguise.
It might have wrinkles, indicating a recent tryst.
Also, I may wear a fedora.
I will certainly have a lot of hair
falling over the brim of my eyelashes, either because
I'm too busy to cut it
or I don't want anyone looking me in the eyes.
Ominous footsteps echo in an unseen room,
along with distant thunder.
We are unsure of the dialogue in this script.

You watch me lean into the wet, shining street
and peer, nervous, into shadows.
Am I looking for you?
Or the man with a gun?
Either way, I'm holding tickets to Paris.
Care to join me?
I would light a cigarette
except for the damn rain. My lipstick
in this lighting is darker than blood,
and my hands won't stop shaking.

## Happily Ever After

Every night we climb into the same bed.
There is nothing better than love's beginning:
all the poems say so. Less is said
of the long afterwards,
after that shiver has gone still
as my looking glass.

Somehow living with you I feel
more solitary in my skin,
as if everything beneath it
is protected from your touch,
that this ring on my finger
is a talisman of separation.
I feel like the moon's fierce teeth,
remote and terrible,
enchanted into silence.

Do you think love lasts longer
when one side is unrequited?
If you were changed into a bird
by a wicked queen, again,
or I, encased in a coffin of glass
or a castle of thorns,
would we regain our old magic?
But all I get in answer is your quiet snore.

The moon hunts white stags
with silver arrows. She catches
the reflection of her pale limbs
in the water, uninterrupted by men,
their strange harsh voices,
their craving arms.

# The Monster Speaks: It's Not So Bad

Being a monster, really. It slows down traffic
from neighbors and I'm finally getting the respect
I deserve. For years they snickered behind curtains
when I passed by, but now they cross themselves

(I think in reverence.) They clutch babies
to their chests and wail. They lay their hands
over the eyes of the dead. I can peek
in their windows, raid the pantries, curl

up in their attics for a night. I found a picture
they carved of me in black slate.
It wasn't a very good likeness, but they meant
well. Children dream of me.

I am no longer lonely, I enjoy the dark,
the click-click of my claws against glass,
the way my tail sparkles in moonlight. Even
this new voice bewitches me. If you put

your ear on my chest, you can hear
the new, unfamiliar thumps of four hearts,
each stronger than the last. Touch the skin
between wing-bones, the delicate eyelids.

In this body I've become myself again.
As I circle the castle, the song that scrapes
my throat agitates the stars themselves.
The music stings your lungs like the burning of stone.

## Procne and Philomel, at the End

### I.

He didn't finish me; at least not the way
he meant to, locking me in that cold room,
bleeding from the mouth,
thinking of my lost voice.

He couldn't stop me
from telling my story,
even with this stump of tongue,
images blooming like cherry blossoms from my fingertips.

It was the gods that freed me
at last from his hawk-like grip,
gave me another voice, garbled and forlorn.

I didn't think it would end here, in the treetops,
one more song silenced. Keep your eye
on the sparrow falling, falling
like the numbered hairs from your head.

### II.

No one noticed me
as a nest of trinkets grew
around my son's tiny grave,
a blue blanket, pink peonies
with blooms curling like infant feet.

Only nightmares pursue me,
sometimes my son's blood on my hands,
I can't understand my own voice,
my husband stares at me like I am nothing
but an animal.

No one searches for my name
among the stars, "bad wife," "bad mother."
Just one more swallow haunting the temple
with her lazy circles.

When lightning strikes, the smell
like blood still in my mouth when I try
to sing Itylus I lost I lost

## The Conversation

I am an avenging goddess, she said, severely.
What about that do you not understand?

I need you, he said. Even without your costumes.
I lie in the dark and think of you. Every night more.

I eat men like you for breakfast. Her right hand gripped
a sword. I've forgotten how to make my lips do anything but sneer.

I could make you French toast instead, he offered.
He was blond and easy on the eyes.

There is no happy ending for us. You've seen the stories—
in the end I'd be bent over your slain body,

miss the gunshot, the final blow. But think, he said, how sad,
all that you're missing—the slow sunny afternoons in pajamas,

maybe a cat—or an African pygmy hedgehog—on the couch.
Trips to the grocery store. Bad movies.

Anyway, she said, I'm late. She picked up a handbag full of arrows.
Please try not to disclose my secret identity. I'll see you later.

He pretended not to care as her shadow lengthened in the doorway.
She pretended not to notice the sudden heaviness of her sword.

## Persephone Thinks of Leaving the Suburbs

I miss Sicily:
the blood oranges and olive groves,
sunshine and seaweed.

Here, my garden grows drowsy,
out of the light: white poppies,
Lenten Rose, bleeding hearts.

The neighbors aren't unpleasant,
their faces are mild and pale,
their dreams stunted, undemanding.

Like the herbs I coax out of this cold ground:
valerian, verbena. I work without gloves,
ripping my cuticles, staining my fingertips with mud.

Even the weeds here are sickly.
Lavender, rosemary—the scents seem diluted, bluer
now than during my visits home.

I dream of fields lush with gypsum,
blossoms of chrysolite and blue lace agate,
opals like ghosts of former jewels

that creep across the membranes of caves
like shadows. How strange for spring to survive all these months
underground, shrouded in the breath of the dead.

## Here There Be Monsters

You were always trying to sneak
under my long skirts, though I told you
the best thing about me was my hair,
its writhing mass of gold and glitter,
followed by my voice. Still you wove
intricate fantasies of my mermaid tail twitching
beside you, the shine of it in your eyes.
I told you I could not join you
for a walk in the park, I could not give you
children. But you kept combing my hair,
stroking my back, as if this would reassure me,
give me a reason to stay.

Let me sing you to sleep:
Don't you know, son of earth, that I am not
one of yours? There is no dance we could do
together. So go home to your wives or lovers,
but continue to sketch homages to me
in the corners of your maps and diaries,
go sit in bars with other sailors
and swear to them you once knew me.

Why do you keep creating us half-human,
with bat wings, dragon scales, luminous green skin,
as if you can't appreciate ordinary women anymore,
as if you fear what lies beneath?

# Women in Refrigerators

"Not every woman in comics has been killed, raped, depowered, crippled, turned evil, maimed, tortured, contracted a disease…but given the following list…it's hard to think up exceptions…"

Gail Simone, comic book author, from *The Women In Refrigerators* web site

You never rescue us, always ten minutes too late.
You find the note on the counter about a surprise in the fridge.
And in the next frame the surprise, the punch line:
Susan or Sally hacked into pieces, left to chill.

If by some chance we do grow powerful or popular,
we are blinded, kidnapped by demons, put into wheelchairs,
impregnated by rape. Our memories are stolen. We lose
children and husbands, are condemned to asylums.

If we're lucky, we might become the villainess.
Frankly, we'll take the spandex, content to play
the supporting role as long as it buys us time;
until someone comes along to free us,

to write us back to our real selves:
our dormant wings undamaged, injuries healed,
we rise once more to command the wind, put on armor,
race against the slivered edge of night.

## She Complains About the Mockingbird

Outside her window, it keeps her awake
with lavish songs too loud for pre-dawn

dreaming. So she drank too much last night,
and danced too long, kissed Bill afterwards.

Now she is cursing the innocent bird
who after all is not to blame, and is only

working hard, same as the rest of us, defending
her home land, attracting a mate, simply trying

to make a cohesive whole out of the fragments
of car horns blaring, the dogs, their woof language,

the trees, cursing, cats and catbirds, all the songs
she has heard on her travels. So don't be too hard

on her, this morning, lady, you still in the red dress
with your smear of eye makeup, a trace of glitter,

while you stumble towards the sun
of orange juice in your glass.

## Instructions to my Successor in the Event of my Death

Put me in a glass coffin.
Dress me in my tiara, a swimsuit
and high-heeled slippers of fur or glass.
Float me away from dragons,
sputtering and elderly,
away from towers ringed with thorny hedges,
away at last from my husband, quiet as the grave.

Leaving behind
girl infants fat as roses, pale as snow
visiting them as hazel and birch trees,
or vengeful and furious doves.
No trail of bread crumbs
this time.

Brittle as sticks
we go on dying
red lipstick
still staining our mouths.
In silver boxes
our mothers' voices
rattle like combs.

## The Slayer Asks for Time Off

It's hard enough just trying to pick out
the miniskirt that matches my platform jellies

but as you know, the cute-as-a-button cheerleader
must also answer to the darkest demons

(if you've watched any animé, you know this drill
already— how I'll prowl through corridors

looking fragile in the shadows, how the monster
grabs my ponytail from behind and I'm

knocked, momentarily, off my tiny feet
but will spring up, brandishing the medieval sword

hiding in my teddy-bear backpack.)
And don't think it doesn't get boring, the back flips

and the bite marks and perfectly timed execution
of one more stake through the heart. I'm tired of wiping blood

off my jeans, the adrenaline rush in graveyards.
Just once I'd like to take the night off, maybe

be the damsel in distress, instead of always,
always, wearing the armor and carrying the flag.

## *With You Rubbing My Feet*

warm, I almost forget
the ugly color of the sky,
the worm trails of planes.

Under the rough pads of skin on your fingertips,
you calm the blue pulse of my nervous white feet,
their frenetic tapping, the rush of blood

in my ears and stomach.
You breathe slowly, so do I, and right now
you are the one I want to write a poem for,

maybe a poem about waking to a perfect breakfast,
maybe of strawberries
tiny as baby teeth.

## The Dead Girl Speaks

The dead girl at the end of the picture must wear flowers
in her hair. If there were no flowers, we would have to
admit the ugliness of mortality.

Everyone loves the dead girl after she's dead, without the sins
of blood and beating heart. No choke marks are visible
on her neck.

The dead girl floats gently down a stream, carried by fairies.
No one remembers how cold that stream is, how it burns
your feet with its coldness.

The dead girl would have liked to be the one holding the
gun. She wishes she had studied Xiao Lin Do, or how to
throw a knife, wishes for one more chance to feel against
her skin the cotton shirt of dirt and sweat.

The dead girl knows that men love her now that she is dead.
She remembers how it felt to press her hands against the
flatness of a hard stomach, the muscular thigh, and how
it cost her.

The dead girl had children ripped from her body before her
burial. She wanted to be buried beside them, like a nest
full of eggs.

In the end we envy the dead girl, because she is so pretty.
Because she is so pretty, she is dead. Mothers, scar your
little girl's faces so that no prince will pick them from the
villagers. Girls, put down the lipstick; why attract all that
light?

The dead girl says, when the spotlight's on you, they never let
you forget it.

## Notes on Poems

*"Alice, in Darkness"*

Lewis Carroll's Alice has inspired a wonderfully macabre video game and a series of famous Manga novels and animé characters. She makes frequent appearances in comic books.

*"Leda's Mother Warns Her"*

Leda, the Queen of Sparta, was raped by Zeus who visited her in the form of a swan, and had children born from eggs, including Helen of Troy.

*"Remembering Philomel"*

The myth of Philomel and Procne is best told in Ovid's *Metamorphoses*. Philomel and Procne were sisters, princesses of Athens. When Tereus came to visit their father's kingdom, he was given Procne's hand in marriage (Philomel was considered too young.) Tereus became obsession with Philomel, so after marrying Procne and fathering a son, Itylus, he went back to Athens under the guise of bringing Philomel back to visit Procne. But Tereus took her to a cabin in a remote forest instead and raped her repeatedly. When she threatened to tell her sister, he cut out her tongue and left her to die. She sewed the rape scene onto a tapestry which she sent into Tereus' castle. Procne found out what happened and rescued her sister, vowing revenge against her husband. Procne and Philomel murdered Itylus, Procne and Tereus' only child, and fed him to Tereus. When he chased after them, the gods changed Philomel into a nightingale, Procne into a swallow, and Tereus into a sea hawk. The red on the chest of the swallow was said to be a blood stain from the murder of Itylus. The nightingale in T.S. Eliot's *The Waste Land* sings "Tereu, Tereu..." in reference to these events. Marianne Moore also refers to the mythic nightingale in her collage poem "Marriage."

*"Okay, Ophelia"*

After killing herself because of Hamlet's erratic behavior towards her, Ophelia gained new life as the star of many books and art works, kind of a fetishized-beautiful-dead-girl object. Recently, there were several books about women in adolescence invoking this mythic archetype of the teenage girl as victim called *Reviving Ophelia, Ophelia Speaks*, etc. The last line refers to Isaiah 41:15.

*"Female Comic Book Superheroes II: When Catholic School Girls Strike Back"*

Refers to an incident on October 31, 2003, when a man, a known sexual predator, was chased through the streets of Philadelphia by an angry crowd of Catholic high school girls, who attacked him so severely he required medical attention before he was taken to jail.

*"Wonder Woman Dreams of the Amazon"*

Wonder Woman was named Diana, the Roman name for Artemis. Her origins in comic book lore indicate that she was born on Paradise Island, raised by a group of Amazon women, and eventually sent to the USA to fight Nazis, among other evil-doers. In the seventies-era television series, Wonder Woman changed from her pedestrian identity of Diana Prince to her "super" self by spinning around. In Greek myth, Hippolyta was a queen of the Amazons who was kidnapped and married against her will to the Greek king Theseus, with Heracles in tow. Theseus eventually decided he wanted to marry someone else, and in different versions of the myth, Hippolyta was killed by Theseus' men when she stormed her husband's second wedding, or by Heracles.

*"When Red Becomes the Wolf"*

"Lupus" in Latin means "Wolf." "Lupae" in Latin meant "She-Wolf," but was also used to mean "Whore" or "Prostitute."

*"Allerleirauh Reveals Her True Self to the Prince"*

Allerleirauh, loosely translated, means "coat of many furs"
in German. This fairy tale (and its French counterpart,
"Donkeyskin") resembles several stories of female saints who
lived between the 2nd and 12th centuries.

*"Persephone and the Prince Meet Over Drinks"*

The Persephone myth involves the young daughter of Demeter,
Persephone, who was kidnapped by the God of the dead, Hades,
while she was picking flowers. Because she ate six pomegranate
seeds while she was in Hades, Zeus decreed that she must spend
six months of each year with her husband in Hades, and six
months with her mother Demeter on earth.

*"Lament for the Seal Wife's Daughter"*

This poem's title and contents are adapted from a traditional folk
tale of the Orkney Islands, sometimes called "The Selkie Wife,"
other times, "The Goodman of Wastness." "Selkie" can refer
to seals or to half-seal, half-human creatures. Similar tales can
be found in Scottish folk tales and folk tales from the Shetland
Islands.

*"Daphne, Older"*

The Greek god Apollo fell in love with the river-nymph Daphne,
but she wanted no part of him. She tried to outrun him but when
that didn't work, she asked her father, the god of the river, to save
her. He changed her into a laurel tree.

*"The Fairy Melusine's Reproach"*

Melusine was believed to have lived in the 10th century in French
Bretagne; she supposedly introduced locals to concepts of
architecture and agriculture. Her name and image can still be
found on churches, wells and castles in the area, and the image

of a half-woman, half-serpent is sometimes found on agricultural products of the region to this day. For instance, if you buy honey in Poitou, it is sometimes labeled "Melu-miel." Luxembourg also claims Melusine and issued a stamp with her image. In legends, she was a half-human, half-fairy being cursed to be a half-serpent on Saturdays. Melusine was wooed by a knight who asked her to marry him; she agreed on the condition that he never visit her on Saturdays. They had many children, each of whom had some monstrous deformity. Eventually, Melusine's mortal husband broke his promise and cursed her in front of his court. In response, she changed into an immortal winged serpent, and still appears, wailing, during the deaths and births of people of her family line. One of their sons burned down a monastery full on monks and had to be put to death. This myth is related to the Celtic myth of the Banshee, the story of the Little Mermaid, and also to the legend of the Lady of the Lake.

*"The Dead Girl Speaks"*

This poem is written after Marvin Bell's "The Dead Man" poems.

## About the Author:

Jeannine Hall Gailey is a Seattle-area journalist who publishes articles on subject matter as varied as how to bake a perfect scone to how to secure your web services application. Her poems have appeared in *The Iowa Review*, *The Columbia Poetry Review*, *Verse Daily*, and *32 Poems*, among others. She has an M.A. in English from the University of Cincinnati and is studying for her MFA at Pacific University in Oregon. Her chapbook, "Female Comic Book Superheroes," is available from Pudding House Press and from her web site, www.webbish6.com. She really does still read comic books at age 32.

# *Acknowledgments*

With many thanks to the editors of these literary journals, in which my work (sometimes in slightly different form) has appeared.

*32 Poems* "While Reading *Glamour* in a Dark Age"

*88* "Breathing In the Asthma Capital"

*The Adirondack Review* "The Villainess"

*The American Poetry Journal* "The Conversation," "She Complains About the Mockingbird" and "Wonder Woman Dreams of the Amazon"

*The Beloit Poetry Journal* "Remembering Philomel"

*Can We Have Our Ball Back* "My Little Brother, In Parts"

*Cranky* "Female Comic Book Superheroes"

*The Columbia Poetry Review* "On Dying Again: Dirge for a Video Game Heroine"

*Diner* "Allerleirauh Reveals Her True Self to the Prince"

*The Evansville Review* "Becoming the Villainess"

*The Iowa Review* "Case Studies in Revenge: Philomel Gives Advice"

*Kaleidowhirl* "Playing Softball with Persephone"

*The Melic Review* "Philomel, at the End"

*Rain Dog* "The Snow Queen"

*Redactions* "Leda's Mother Warns Her"

*The Seattle Review* "The Fairy Melusine's Reproach" and "When Red Becomes the Wolf"

*Verse Daily* "Wonder Woman Dreams of the Amazon"

*Wicked Alice* "Her Nerves"

The following poems: "Moth-Girl," "Spy Girls," "In the Faces of Lichtenstein's Women," "The Snow Queen," "Lament for the Selkie Wife's Daughter," "Stepmother, At the Wedding," "Philomel, at the End," "The Changeling," "She Escapes the Film Noir," "Female Comic Book Superheroes," "Wonder Woman Dreams…," "My Little Brother, In Parts" and "On Dying Again: Dirge for a Video Game Heroine" were published in the chapbook *Female Comic Book Superheroes* by Pudding House Press, 2005.

"Wonder Woman Dreams…" was nominated for a Pushcart Prize in 2005.

Printed in the United States
48576LVS00002B/19